Milly, Mc
and
Billy Buttons

"We may look different
but we feel the same."

On the outskirts of town lived a family of
hares. Billy Buttons was the youngest of three
brothers.

His older brothers could run faster than he could. He always came last.
"The hounds will get you," they teased.

Billy Buttons didn't like coming last.

"You need to practise running and saying I'm the fastest hare in the world," encouraged Milly and Molly when Billy Buttons asked them for help.

Billy Buttons ran to the top of the hill
and back again.

"I'm the fastest hare in the world," he said.

"Believe it and one day you will be," said Milly and Molly.

Before long Billy Buttons began catching up to
his brothers. But he still came last.
"The hounds will get you," they teased.

Billy Buttons ran to the top of the next hill and
back again.

"I'm the fastest hare in the world," he said.

"Believe it and one day you will be," said Milly and Molly.

Billy Buttons was catching up to his brothers.
But he still came last.
"The hounds will get you," they teased.

Billy Buttons ran to the top of the faraway hill and back again.

"I'm the fastest hare in the world," he said.

"Believe it and one day you will be," said Milly and Molly.

Then the day arrived that all hares wait for –
the day the fastest hare in the world
is decided.

Billy Buttons and his brothers ran off to join
the start line.

Billy Buttons was catching up to his brothers.
But still he came last.
"The hounds will get you," they teased.

Suddenly, Billy Buttons heard something behind him. Was it the hounds coming to get him?

He began to run faster and faster.
"I'm the fastest hare in the world," he said,
over and over again.

Billy Buttons reached the start line as the gun went off.

He ran faster and faster and faster.
"I'm the fastest hare in the world," he said,
over and over and over again.

And he was!

Billy Buttons crossed the finish line first.

"The hounds won't get me now," he teased his brothers.